SEASONS

AUTUMN

Stephanie Turnbull

 An Appleseed Editions book

Paperback edition 2015

First published in 2014 by Franklin Watts
338 Euston Road, London NW1 3BH

Created by Appleseed Editions Ltd,
Well House, Friars Hill, Guestling,
East Sussex TN35 4ET

Designed by Hel James
Edited by Mary-Jane Wilkins

A CIP record for this book is available from the
British Library

ISBN 978 1 4451 3167 2

Dewey Classification: 508.2

Photo acknowledgements
t = top, b = bottom
page 1 odze/Shutterstock; page 3 iStockphoto/
Thinkstock; 5 background iStockphoto/Thinkstock,
inset Poznyakov/Shutterstock; 6 Paul Aniszewski/
Shutterstock; 7 Ingram Publishing/Thinkstock;
8 iStockphoto/Thinkstock; 9 Stockbyte/Thinkstock;
0 Ron Chapple Studios/Thinkstock; 11t SAJE/
Shutterstock, b iStockphoto/Thinkstock;
12 iStockphoto/Thinkstock; b Medioimages/
Photodisc; 14 iStockphoto/Thinkstock;
15 CreativeNature.nl/Shutterstock; 16-17 Myotis/
Shutterstock; 18 iStockphoto/Thinkstock;
19 Tom Grundy/Shutterstock; 20 JeniFoto/
Shutterstock; 21 iStockphoto/Thinkstock;
22 background Shunsuke Yamamoto Photography/
Thinkstock; 23t Hemera/Thinkstock, b Kai Wong/
Shutterstock
Cover Ingram Publishing/Thinkstock

Printed in China

Franklin Watts is a division of Hachette Children's Books,
an Hachette UK company
www.hachette.co.uk

Contents

It's autumn!

Fat orange
pumpkins are
ripe and ready.

Shorter days

Our autumn months are September, October and November.

The sun comes up later every morning and sets earlier every evening.

Sunlight is weaker,
so autumn can be chilly.
Dress warmly!

Wet and dry

Many autumn mornings
are misty. Glittering
drops of dew cover grass,
leaves and spider webs.

Some days are wild,
wet and windy.

Other days are still,
sunny and perfect
for playing outdoors.

Taking a break

Plants stop growing in autumn. Some die, but others have roots alive underground.

These flowers bloom then die back.

Leaves turn
golden yellow,
flaming red
or rusty brown.

9

Leaves everywhere!

Gusts of wind send dry leaves fluttering to the ground.

Winged seeds whirl
through the air.
Next year these
may start growing
into new trees.

Fat mushrooms sprout
in damp piles of leaves.

Fruit and food

Raspberries and blackberries are fat and juicy in autumn.

Spiky green fruits on horse chestnut trees protect the big, glossy seeds inside.

It's time for farmers
to gather their crops.
This is called harvest.

Munch, munch

Animals gobble all the nuts, seeds and berries they can find. Winter is coming and soon there will be less to eat. Squirrels store extra nuts in safe places.

Bye bye!

Some animals don't wait for winter – they leave instead! These geese are flying south to warmer places. Their journey may take weeks.

They will come back in spring.

Yawn...

Many animals find safe places to sleep through the winter.

Mice curl up tightly in cosy nests.

Insects such as butterflies look for cracks or piles of logs to hide in.

Bats hang upside down
in quiet caves.

Autumn fun

Festivals in autumn
celebrate harvest
and all the crops
that have grown.

Halloween is a time
to dress up and have
a spooky party with
your friends!

Did you know...?

When we have autumn,
it is spring in the southern
half of the world.

Trees called evergreens don't
lose their leaves in autumn.

Every autumn, birds
called Arctic terns
fly from the
North Pole all the
way to the South Pole!

At Chinese harvest
festivals, people
eat sweet pastries
called mooncakes.

Useful words

autumn
The time of year, called a season, after summer and before winter.

dew
Water in the air that gathers on cool surfaces at night.

crops
Plants such as wheat and corn that are grown by farmers for food.

roots
Plant parts that store water and food from soil to keep the plant alive.

Index